THE *COBRA*

BY
CARL R. GREEN
WILLIAM R. SANFORD

EDITED BY
DR. HOWARD SCHROEDER
Professor in Reading and Language Arts
Dept. of Elementary Education
Mankato State University

PRODUCED AND DESIGNED BY
BAKER STREET PRODUCTIONS
Mankato, MN

CRESTWOOD HOUSE
Mankato, Minnesota

LIBRARY OF CONGRESS CATALOGING IN PUBLICATION DATA
Green, Carl R.
  The cobra.

  (Wildlife, habits & habitats)
  SUMMARY: Examines the six species of cobras, their physical appearance, habitats, life cycle, and relationship to man.
  1. Cobras--Juvenile literature. (1. Cobras) I. Sanford, William R. (William Reynolds). II. Schroeder, Howard. III. Baker Street Productions. IV. Title. V. Series.
QL666.064G74   1985   597.96   85-19460
ISBN 0-89686-266-6 (lib. bdg.)

International Standard Book Number:	Library of Congress Catalog Card Number:
Library Binding 0-89686-289-5	85-19469

ILLUSTRATION CREDITS:

Cris Crowley/Tom Stack & Assoc.: Cover, 38
Nadine Orabona/Stock Concepts: 4, 19, 40, 45
John C. Murphy/Tom Stack & Assoc.: 7
Leonard Lee Rue III: 8, 15, 20
Brian Parker/Tom Stack & Assoc.: 11
Tom Stack/Tom Stack & Assoc.: 12, 16, 28, 34
Bob Williams: 22-23, 26
Gary Milburn/Tom Stack & Assoc.: 24-25, 31

CRESTWOOD·HOUSE
Hwy. 66 South, Box 3427
Mankato, MN 56002-3427

TABLE OF CONTENTS

Introduction: The cobra and the snake charmer ...5
Chapter I: The cobra in close-up 8
   A large and dangerous family
   Six kinds of cobras
   Who needs legs
   A look inside
   Senses geared to a snake's life
   Fangs and venom
Chapter II: Cobras live in many parts of Asia and Africa......................................19
   Typical habitats
   Hunting for a varied diet
   Many natural enemies
   Cobras don't look for trouble
Chapter III: The life cycle of an Indian Cobra ...29
   When cobras mate
   Nests and eggs
   Leaving the egg
   The cobra grows up
   The cycle is complete
Chapter IV: The cobra in today's world.........35
   Cobras appear in many myths
   Worshipping the cobra
   The cobra in the West
Chapter V: The man who's immune to cobra venom 41
   A lifesaving plane flight
   Milking a cobra
   Venom has many uses
   Time for seventy-one?
Map 46
Index/Glossary 47

An Indian cobra flares its hood.

INTRODUCTION:

The snake charmer walked barefoot into a village in southern India. The orange turban on his head and his striped shirt told everyone that he was from the Jogi tribe. The snake charmer, whose name was Naga, carried a reed basket in one hand.

Ten-year-old Pandit Ramu joined the village people who were following Naga. When the crowd was big enough, the snake charmer sat down to begin his show. The people watched the reed basket with special attention.

Naga began playing a song on his wooden flute. He swayed back and forth in time to the music. The excitement grew. Finally, Naga reached out and took the lid off the basket. A full-grown cobra rose up to face the snake charmer.

Only the top third of the cobra's six-foot (1.8 m) length showed above the basket. Its brown, slender body was marked with narrow white rings. The cobra sensed danger. It spread its neck into a broad, flat hood. The eyeglass markings on the back of its hood showed clearly.

The bright light seemed to dazzle the snake. It swayed back and forth in rhythm to the music. To Pandit, it looked as though the cobra was dancing to Naga's tune. Each time he speeded up or slowed down, the snake stayed with him. Suddenly, in one lightning motion the cobra struck! Naga was ready. He pulled back slightly, and the deadly fangs missed their target. The cobra rose up again, still swaying to the music.

When the show was over, Naga forced the snake back into the basket and put the lid on. The villagers gave him coins to pay for the show.

That night, Pandit told his father about the Jogi snake charmer. Dr. Ramu was a teacher, and Pandit was sure he knew everything.

Dr. Ramu laughed. "So, you saw the snake dance to the music, did you? Therefore, old Naga is a true snake charmer, right?"

Pandit nodded. He guessed that he was about to learn that the snake charmer had tricked him.

"First, remember that cobras are like all snakes," Dr. Ramu said. "They don't have ears, so they can't hear the music. The cobra simply swayed in time to Naga's movements. That's the cobra's way of warning its enemies to watch out. Second, that cobra was almost certainly harmless. Many snake charmers break off the snake's fangs. Some even sew the cobra's mouth shut!"

"Doesn't that hurt the cobra?" Pandit protested.

"Of course. Either way, the cobra will die soon," Dr. Ramu told him. "Then Naga will go out and catch another one. That's when there's real danger. Naga isn't immune to snake venom. If he gets bitten, he may die."

Pandit thought about what his father had said. He knew that some Hindu people worship the cobra. They think it's a symbol of one of their gods. But he also knew that the bite of the giant king cobra can kill an elephant. "I guess I better get busy and find out some more about cobras," he told himself.

Hindu people worship the cobra.

CHAPTER ONE:

The first snakes appeared on earth thousands of years ago. Naturalists think that they developed from a type of lizard that lived underground. Legs and ears were of little value in that dark and narrow habitat.

In time the snakes came back to the surface. They made themselves at home almost everywhere. Except for a few islands, only the polar regions and the deep oceans don't have snakes. All were excellent predators, but one branch of the family developed a special way of hunting. The venomous snakes killed their prey with poison.

Venomous snakes, like this forest cobra, use poison to kill their prey.

A large and dangerous family

One large sub-family of venomous snakes is known as the *elapidae*. Elapids are found on every continent but Europe. The coral snakes of North America are elapids, as are sea snakes and mambas. All elapids have short, fixed fangs at the front of their mouths. By contrast, members of the viper family have long fangs that fold back when they close their mouths. Most elapids are slender, brightly colored snakes.

The best known elapids are a group of snakes that naturalists call *Naja*—the cobras. A true cobra is a slender snake with a wide, flat head. It has smooth scales that can be shiny or dull according to the species. The typical cobra's hollow fangs carry a venom five times more deadly than that of most rattlesnakes. Cobras are also known for raising the front part of their body off the ground when they sense danger. They spread the ribs in their necks into a wide, flat "hood" at the same time.

Six kinds of cobras

Of the six true cobras, five live in Africa. The sixth, with its ten sub-species, is found in Asia. Several other elapids have *Naja*-like hoods and habits, but are not true cobras.

The Egyptian cobra *(Naja haje)* is found in the Nile valley, in parts of the Middle East, and along the east coast of Africa. This snake is heavier than most cobras, and grows to a length of eight feet (2.4 m) or more. It is usually brown or black, with specks of lighter color. Legend says that the famous Queen Cleopatra let an Egyptian cobra bite her when she decided to kill herself.

The forest cobra *(Naja melanoleuca)* lives in the rain forests of Africa. Forest cobras can grow to nine feet (2.7 m) or more. These large snakes are glossy black on top and white underneath. The forest cobra can raise two-thirds of its length off the ground. That means a full-grown forest cobra can look a tall hunter eye-to-eye!

The cape cobra *(Naja nivea)* is found only in the dry areas of southern Africa. These small cobras grow to about five feet (1.5 m), and are yellow to golden-brown in color. Cape cobras have the most deadly of all cobra venoms.

Spitting cobras are found in many parts of Africa. They use their venom in an unusual way. When hunting, they "spit" venom at their prey. Blinded by the venom, the prey animal is an easy victim. Spitting cobras also use this method to escape from a predator. Their spray of venom can blind a lion as much as ten feet (3 m) away. Black-necked cobras *(Naja nigricollis)* are spitters who grow to over five feet (1.5 m) in length. Mostly black on top and light-colored below, they have

The spitting cobra is one of five cobras found in Africa.

a black band at the throat that gives them their name. The smaller Mozambique spitting cobra *(Naja mossabica)* is pale grey to olive on top and pink below. The ringhals *(Hemachatus haemachatus)* are spitters who display a hood like the true cobras. These black, five-foot (1.5 m) snakes also play ''dead.'' To escape danger, they sometimes lie on their backs with their tongues hanging out.

The ten sub-species of the Asiatic cobra *(Naja naja)* range from the Philippines to the Middle East. The best-known Asiatic cobra is the Indian cobra *(N. naja naja)*. Also known as the spectacled cobra for the eyeglass

The "king cobra" is not a true cobra.

marks on its hood, the Indian cobra is usually a dark brown with light rings. These cobras grow to six feet (1.8 m) or more. Snake charmers usually use the Indian cobra in their shows.

The king cobra *(Ophiophagus hannah)* is not a true cobra, despite its name. It is a hooded elapid, however, and it is the largest of all venomous snakes. King cobras average over twelve feet (3.7 m) in length. The record king cobra was over eighteen feet (5.6 m) long! These giants can be black, olive-brown, or grey. Their habitat ranges from India eastward to southern China and the Philippines.

Who needs legs?

Nature did a good job of equipping cobras for their lives as predators. Their strong bodies have flexible backbones and several hundred pairs of ribs. They can easily cross rough ground, swamps, desert sand, and heavy jungle. When necessary, cobras can swim a river, climb a tree, or slip into an animal's underground burrow.

The cobra uses its strong muscles and belly scales to move forward. As the muscles lift its body, the belly scales push back against rough spots on the ground. To an observer, the snake seems to be gliding across the ground in a series of S-curves.

The scales wear out quickly, and must be replaced

three or four times a year. The cobra does this by shedding its skin. When it's time to shed, the snake rubs its nose on the ground. The old skin comes loose from the lower jaw. After some more rubbing, the cobra finally crawls out of its old skin. The new scales show the cobra's colors at their brightest.

A look inside

Naturalists sometimes think of the cobra as a very efficient eating machine. Its body has been designed to take in and digest large meals. The jaws open wide enough to fit around animals larger than the snake itself. Once swallowed, its digestive system breaks the animal down into the nutrients the snake needs to survive.

The cobra's organs are designed to fit its long, slender shape. The cobra has one long lung, for example, instead of two. The lung also stores air to help keep the snake afloat when it is swimming. Similarly, the cobra's rather primitive heart has only three valves instead of the usual four. A vent near the tail allows both sexes to get rid of waste materials and to mate. The female also lays her eggs through the vent. Since their sex organs are hidden inside the body, it is difficult to tell a male from a female.

Like all reptiles, cobras have a serious problem: they are cold-blooded animals. This means they cannot control their body temperature. As a result, most cobras are found in warm climates that don't get colder than sixty degrees F (15 degrees C). If the weather turns cold, they become sluggish and inactive. Too much heat, however, can raise their body temperature high enough to kill them.

Senses geared to a snake's life

A cobra's senses are different than those of most other animals. For one thing, cobras don't have external ears, so they cannot "hear" airborne sounds. Cobras do have

Cobras can't hear sounds, but they can feel vibrations.

an inner ear that responds to vibrations. They can't "hear" your footsteps, but their bodies can "feel" you coming down the path! In addition, their skin is highly sensitive to touch.

The cobra's eyesight is also limited. Naturalists believe that the cobra can see objects clearly only when they are close by. Snakes don't have eyelids, so the cobra's eye is covered by a clear shield that is part of its skin. The round pupil closes to a vertical slit in bright light.

Snakes do not have eyelids.

The cobra finds its prey through its highly developed sense of smell and taste. If you watch a cobra, you'll see its forked tongue flick out every few seconds. The sticky tips of the tongue pick up tiny bits of matter from the air and ground. When the tongue retracts, a special sensing organ on the roof of the mouth "taste-smells" the material. Naturalists call this the organ of Jacobson. The cobra uses its nose only for breathing.

Fangs and venom

Because a cobra's fangs are fixed in place in the upper jaw, they are quite short. An adult Indian cobra's fangs are about a quarter of an inch (6 mm) long. By comparison, a large rattlesnake's fangs may be a full inch (25 mm) long. Each sharp, hollow fang is connected to a poison gland in the cobra's cheek. When the cobra strikes, cheek muscles force the venom through the fangs and into the prey. After it strikes, the cobra hangs on. It chews at the wound and injects more and more venom.

A full "load" of venom for an Indian cobra is about three hundred milligrams (that's only .01 oz.). The cobra injects a fifth of its supply of venom when it strikes. That's about sixty milligrams—but twenty milligrams can kill most humans. The yellowish venom works on the cobra's victims in two ways. First, the poison affects the nervous system. Victims have trouble

17

breathing, feel sleepy, and can't move their muscles properly. In severe cases, their hearts may stop beating. Second, the venom breaks down tissue and causes bleeding inside the body. This process makes it easier for the cobra to digest its prey.

Over half of the people bitten by cobras recover. Treatment with antivenin drugs saves many of these people. In addition, the cobra does not always inject its venom when it bites. Experts guess that the snake can decide whether to release the venom or not. Sometimes, the cobra may have used up most of its venom in earlier strikes.

Spitting cobras have the biggest venom supply of all. When they "spit," the venom shoots out in a thin stream that breaks into a spray of tiny drops. Spitting cobras are accurate up to six feet away (1.8 m), but the venom may travel as far as fifteen feet (4.6 m). The spitting cobra aims for the eyes of its prey. Once the prey is blinded, the cobra moves in for the kill. Herpetologists (naturalists who study reptiles) wear goggles when they work with these snakes in the laboratory!

Herpetologists don't spend all their time in the lab, however. They prefer to study cobras in the snake's own environment. Out in the field, they have a chance to see how the cobra has adapted to life in many parts of Asia and Africa.

CHAPTER TWO:

The cobra has adapted to a wide variety of habitats. The people of Africa and Asia find these venomous snakes living everywhere from dry, arid regions to dripping rain forests. Cobras can be found in swamps and woodlands and rice paddies. Sometimes, people find them living in their backyards!

Typical habitats

The Egyptian cobra prefers hot and dry places. It roams the dusty edges of the Sahara desert, where its

The Egyptian cobra lives in areas that are hot and dry.

brown, speckled skin blends in with the desert soil. By contrast, the black-necked spitting cobra is found in the humid climate of central Africa's rain forest. A lover of damp places, the forest cobra spends part of its time in the water. This excellent swimmer feeds on fish and frogs as well as on land animals.

The forest cobra likes damp areas.

In Asia, cobras can be found in every habitat, from thick jungles to city parks. Indian cobras show up in rice paddies, gardens, farm sheds, and even on village streets. They generally stay away from humans, but the animals they hunt often live around farms and villages. Indian farmers, for example, value cobras for their help in keeping rats under control. After a night's hunting, the snakes often hide out in old termite nests or in hollow logs.

The deadly king cobras, by contrast, stay well hidden. They prefer dense jungle areas, often near water. Strong and agile, they are good climbers and excellent swimmers. These giant snakes feed during the day as well at night—on other snakes! King cobras eat poisonous and non-poisonous snakes alike. As with all cobras, the king cobra's digestive system takes care of any venom found in its prey. Snake venom is deadly only when it enters the blood stream.

Hunting for a varied diet

Cobras eat meat, not plants. They feed on rats, mice, birds, lizards, frogs, and small fish. Cobras will also climb trees to steal the eggs from a bird's nest. Liquids aren't important to their diet. Snakes don't sweat, and

Cobras are meat eaters.

they lose very little water in their bodily wastes. They get all the fluids they need from their prey.

Unlike the king cobra, true cobras do not hunt for other snakes. A large Indian cobra will sometimes swallow a smaller one by accident, however. If both snakes grab one end of a large rat, the larger snake may eat both the rat and the smaller cobra!

When a cobra senses prey nearby, it raises its body and spreads its hood. This is its attack-defense posture. The cobra usually sways back and forth as it prepares to strike. It may also make a hissing noise. Then with a quick forward lunge, the cobra buries its fangs in the unlucky animal. Once bitten, small animals die quickly from the venom.

Because they can't bite off chunks of meat, cobras must swallow their victims whole. The cobra begins by stretching its jaws wide enough to fit around the dying animal. Slowly, it works the food back into its body, in the same way you put a tight sock on your foot. If something disturbs the cobra, it may eject the food and take up its attack-defense posture. After the danger passes, the snake returns to finish its meal.

A cobra prefers to eat smaller animals every day or so. A cobra that has swallowed a large meal cannot move very well. The victim's body makes a large bulge in the snake's middle. When that happens, the snake crawls back to a hiding place and waits for its meal to be digested.

Cobras go to a hiding place to digest a victim's body.

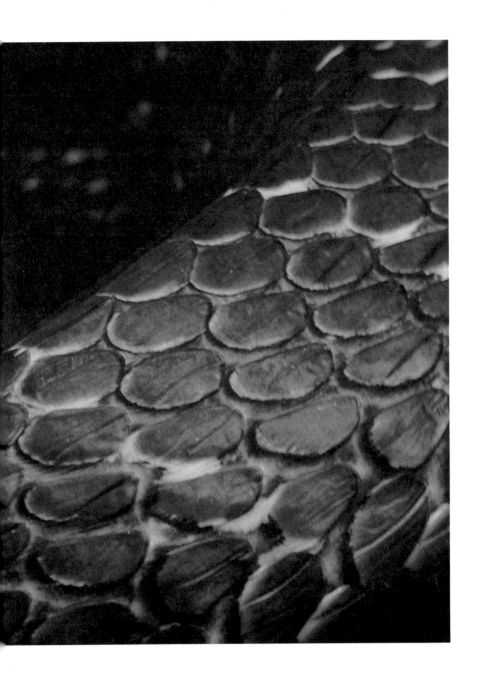

many natural enemies

Can any animal fight a cobra—and win? The answer is yes. Cobras fall victim to such animals as the mongoose, the secretary bird, and the wild pig. Some eagles and hawks also feed on cobras.

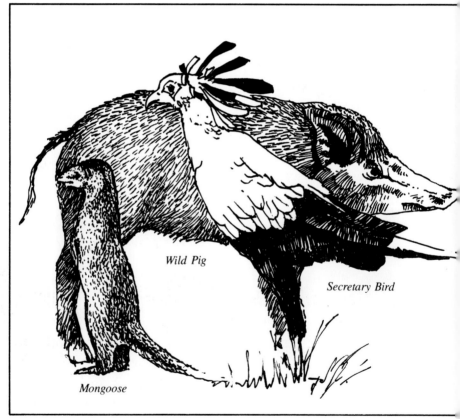

Wild Pig

Secretary Bird

Mongoose

These animals can fight the cobra and win.

Rudyard Kipling, a famous British author, wrote many stories about life in India. One of his tales is about "Rikki-Tikki-Tavi," the mongoose. In the story, Rikki saves a family from a large Indian cobra. In real life, these cat-sized members of the weasel family prefer to hunt smaller animals. If it does fight a cobra, however, the mongoose is quick enough to dodge the deadly fangs. When the snake is worn out, the mongoose darts in and bites the snake on the neck. If the mongoose is bitten, however, the cobra's venom will kill it.

In Africa, the secretary bird and the wild pig feed on cobras and other snakes. The long-legged secretary bird lets the cobra strike harmlessly at its wing feathers. Then the large bird jumps in and tramples the snake. African farmers sometimes keep tame secretary birds around to protect them from snakes. The wild pig hunts cobras in a similar way. The pig waits until the cobra strikes. Before the snake can recover, the pig rushes in and kills the snake with its sharp hooves.

Cobras don't look for trouble

As long as it's left alone, the cobra doesn't go looking for trouble. It does not hunt large animals, and it never hunts humans. When a large animal passes by, a cobra

A cobra will usually "freeze" when danger is near.

will usually freeze in place or crawl away. An Indian cobra may also rise up and turn its back to the danger. Apparently, it hopes to scare the enemy with the large "eyes" on its hood.

But never get too close! A cobra views almost any movement as a possible attack. That's when it rises up into its attack-defense posture, ready to strike. Even newly hatched cobras know how to defend themselves.

CHAPTER THREE:

Studying the cobra in the wild is a tricky business. Even cobras that live near people are hard to find and watch on a regular basis. In addition, herpetologists are always in danger of being bitten by their venomous subjects!

Despite these difficulties, herpetologists have been able to observe the cobra in its natural habitat. They have put together a fairly complete picture of the Indian cobra's life cycle.

When cobras mate

The female cobra lies quietly in the tall grass. It is the end of the rainy season and the mating urge is strong within her. She hasn't eaten for several weeks.

Ten feet away, two golden-brown males spread their hoods and hiss at each other in mock combat. Venom drips from their fangs, but they don't strike. Finally, the smaller male turns and glides back to its den. The females don't mate every year. That means that there are always more males looking for mates than there are females ready to mate. Until the young cobra grows larger, he will be beaten out by older, stronger males.

The larger male's tongue flicks in and out. He turns

and moves slowly toward the female. The two cobras rise to face each other, but they don't spread their hoods. They sway back and forth in what some people have called a courtship dance. Slowly, the dance grows more intense. Their bodies curl around each other. The mating snakes bite and chew on each other in a savage way that may last for hours. Neither snake injects any venom, however.

After the mating is over, the male cobra goes on his way. The female has already chosen a nesting place, Here, in a natural hollow in the ground, she lays her eggs.

Nests and eggs

Herpetologists know that snakes do not care for their young as mammals do. The female Indian cobra, however, stays near the nest to guard her twenty thin-shelled eggs. A mongoose comes too close one morning. Instantly, the female rises to defend her eggs. The mongoose backs away. It's not hungry enough to take on an angry female cobra.

A few miles away, in the deep jungle, a pair of king cobras are working on their own nest. The female piles up bamboo stalks, grass, and branches. When it's finished, the nest is three feet (1 m) across and has two levels. The female lays fifty eggs in the lower "story." Then she coils around the eggs to protect them. Later, she will stand guard from the upper "story." The male king cobra stays nearby, also on guard duty. The eggs don't need the heat from the female's body to hatch. But predators will have to fight two fourteen-foot (4.2 m) king cobras if they want eggs for dinner!

A king cobra defends its nest.

Leaving the egg

Seventy-five days later, the Indian cobra's eggs hatch. The hatching takes three to six hours. Each young cobra has a special egg tooth to cut its way out of the shell. The egg tooth cuts a clean slit in the shell of the two-inch (5 cm) egg. When it's ready, the ten-inch (25 cm) young cobra slips swiftly out of the egg. The other eggs hatch soon afterward. Each young cobra looks like a small copy of its parents.

Once the eggs are hatched, the female leaves. The little ones are on their own. The cobra that hatched first sees movement in a nearby tree. Instantly, it rises up and spreads its tiny hood. Its needle-sharp fangs are already charged with venom. A snake-eating owl swoops down and grabs two of the young cobras. The first cobra strikes at the owl's bony leg, then slips away to safety.

The cobra grows up

The young cobra is five days old and it's hungry. It glides along, tongue flicking, looking for prey. A careless baby rat crosses its path. Instantly, the cobra rises up and strikes. The young snake is clumsy. The baby rat escapes the deadly fangs, but the excited cobra chases it. This time, the fangs find their mark. Three minutes later the baby rat is dead and the cobra opens its mouth to swallow its first meal.

The young cobra has good survival instincts. When a wild pig comes near, it lies very still. Its colors blend in with the grass and leaves. With all its cleverness, life for young cobras is dangerous. Of the twenty cobras hatched in that nest, only four will survive to become adults. Most fall victim to predators. Others die because it is a dry year and food is scarce. The survivors live on grasshoppers and other large insects.

Cobras are not social animals. The young cobra does not seek out the company of other cobras, male or female. After a while, it finds a den in the twisted roots of an old tree. This tree becomes its home base.

One day, a woman from the village sees the cobra slip into its den. The next evening, when it comes out to hunt, she is waiting with a plate of rice and coconut. The woman prays to *Nulla Pambu*—the Good Snake—so the gods will give her a child.

Over the next three years, other people come to pray at the tree. The cobra doesn't eat the food, but it often rises and spreads its hood in front of the watching people. No one thinks that Nulla Pambu is tame, however. One day a child comes too close. The cobra strikes and leaves two deep wounds on the child's leg. The child cries, but the leg doesn't swell up. This time, the cobra didn't use its venom.

The cycle is complete

In its fourth year, the young cobra has grown to ten feet (3 m) in length. A herpetologist who comes to watch can't tell whether the snake is a male or a female. But several male cobras appear as the rainy season ends. They know that Nulla Pambu is a female. She is ready to mate for the first time.

Cobras live about twenty years in the wild, so the female has many years in which to lay eggs. This cobra's life cycle is about to be broken, however. A government bull dozer will soon carve a road through the area. Cobras and human beings will never live together in perfect peace.

Cobras live about twenty years in the wild.

CHAPTER FOUR:

Everyday, over twenty-five people in India are bitten by cobras and other poisonous snakes. If the victims don't receive proper treatment, many will die. You might think that the Indian people would try to kill these dangerous snakes. Instead, many Indians follow a form of snake worship over three thousand years old.

Cobras appear in many myths

Cobras can be found in the myths of many countries. In ancient Egypt, people believed that fire-breathing cobras guarded the four corners of heaven. Their kings wore cobra symbols on their crowns.

In Southeast Asia, the people of Cambodia tell a story of how the cobra got its forked tongue. They say that an eagle once stole a liquid that gave eternal life to the gods. But the eagle spilled a few drops on some blades of grass. The cobra licked up the precious fluid, but cut its tongue on the sharp grass. Thus, the snake gained eternal life at the price of a forked tongue.

The cobra also appears in the legends of the Buddhist religion. Gautama Siddhartha, the Buddha, was once sitting in the desert. A cobra came up and spread its hood to shade him from the hot sun. To thank the cobra, Buddha placed his hand on its hood. The touch created the eyeglass-shaped marks found today on the Indian cobra's hood. Some Buddhists also believe that people who do evil deeds are reborn as cobras.

Worshipping the cobra

In India, many people think of the cobra as a living rebirth of the god Shiva. Cobras are encouraged to live in temples where Shiva is worshipped. The god is often shown wearing a belt made of live cobras.

Women who want children often look for a cobra den. If a cobra is found living in an old termite mound, for example, they bring gifts of rice, milk, coconut, money, and flowers. The women pray to the cobra to help them give birth to many children. They believe that Shiva will answer their prayers.

In the mountains of Burma, young women take part in a religious ceremony with newly caught cobras. After saying special prayers, the women sway back and forth in front of the snakes. The king cobras rise up and strike again and again at the women. Each time, the women dodge just in time. When the snakes are tired and confused, the women lean forward and kiss the snakes on their hoods. Then the snakes are returned to the wild.

A similar festival takes place in July in the Indian village of Shirala. For several weeks before the festival the villagers go out and catch cobras. They put the snakes in clay pots that are kept in cool spots in their houses. On the day of the festival, the people march with their snake pots to the village temple. The owners release the snakes from their pots and hold them by their tails. The other villagers sing and pray to the snake gods. Amazingly, the cobras seldom bite the people who are holding them. A day later, the people set the cobras free.

At home, some Indians set aside a corner of their gardens for a cobra to live in. No one is allowed to cut the grass and bushes in that section of the garden. The people believe that the cobra will bring good fortune to the house.

A family that finds a cobra inside its house isn't as happy. They may call in a Jogi snake charmer to get rid of the unwelcome guest. If the Jogi doesn't find the snake right away, he sometimes plays a trick on the family. He turns loose a snake or two of his own. Then he ''captures'' them and earns the thanks of the frightened people.

The cobra in the West

The people in most Western countries would rather kill cobras than worship them. But herpetologists remind us that poisonous snakes are part of nature's balance. If all of India's cobras were killed, for example, rats would soon be out of control.

Snakes get rid of pests, like rats.

In Europe and the Americas, snake farms keep cobras for display, for study, and for developing antitoxins. The farms often buy cobras from other countries. Cobras are fairly common, so they cost only a few hundred dollars each. Many snake farms and zoos breed their own cobras, however. They also exchange young cobras with other snake farms. The exchanges allow the farms to keep many different cobras on hand.

Cobras adjust quickly to life in a display case. When first let loose, they strike over and over at the glass that separates them from visitors. They stop when they learn that they can't get through the extra-strong glass. After a week or two, the snakes also learn to recognize the keepers who take care of them.

The snake farms work hard to provide a suitable habitat for the cobras. Heat lamps and hot water pipes keep the display cases warm. Fans bring in fresh air, and plants from the snake's wild habitat are grown in the cases. In well-managed snake farms, the snakes live almost normal lives.

Feeding snakes in captivity can be a problem. Many cobras will not eat unless they can catch and kill the prey themselves. If the keepers don't want to feed live animals to the cobras, they try to trick the snakes. They may rub a rat against the meat they want the snake to eat. If the food smells okay, the cobra is likely to swallow the food. In a similar way, chemicals are used to give the proper smell to sausages and other prepared meats. As a rule, cobras are fed only once a week.

There's always danger when the keepers handle the cobras. One herpetologist, who knows all there is to know about snake bites, is William Haast. Haast has been bitten dozens of times by cobras! Let's visit him at his Miami Serpentarium.

Handling a cobra is always dangerous.

CHAPTER FIVE:

Bill Haast was first bitten by a rattlesnake when he was sixteen years old. Since then, he's been bitten by more poisonous snakes than anyone else in history. By the time Haast was seventy, the number of bites was over 140 and still climbing!

Why would anyone take the risk of being bitten by a poisonous snake? For Bill Haast, it's all part of his job. Haast runs the Serpentarium in Miami, Florida. Everyday, crowds of people come to look at the many snakes on display there. The Serpentarium's real purpose, however, is to collect venom from cobras and other deadly snakes.

A lifesaving plane flight

Over the years, Bill Haast has been bitten so often that he's built up an immunity to snake venom. Most of the bites were accidents, but Haast also hurried the process along. Against all advice, he injected himself with a highly poisonous king cobra venom! First, he put a tiny drop of venom in a saltwater solution and injected it. His body showed the symptoms of snake-bite, but he soon felt normal again. Each month he repeated the injection with a stronger dose of venom. At the end of a year he was taking a dose of venom large enough to kill anyone else.

Haast's many bites have turned him into a walking supply of antivenin. With so many antibodies in his blood, he's been called on to fly dozens of rescue missions. Some years ago, for example, a call came from New Orleans. A boy was dying after being bitten at a snake show. An Air Force plane flew Haast to New Orleans, where he donated a pint of his blood. Doctors extracted the antivenin from the blood and injected it into the boy's body. Within a few hours, the boy was out of danger.

Milking a cobra

The cobra venom needed for making antivenin was hard to find in the late 1940's. One ounce of the scarce liquid was worth $1,500. Haast collected cobras and went to work. He picked up each snake by hand and "milked" it for its venom. Even today, there's no better way to "milk" a poisonous snake.

At the Serpentarium you can see Haast or one of his helpers doing this risky job. Let's watch a herpetologist named Barbara. She begins by waving her hand in front of a king cobra. The snake raises up and spreads its hood. It sways from side to side, ready to strike. Swiftly, Barbara reaches out and catches the cobra behind the head. The snake whips back and forth, coiling and uncoiling its powerful body. Because the king cobra is so long, Barbara has a helper ready to hold the snake's tail.

Barbara presses the cobra's fangs over the edge of a glass jar covered by a thin rubber sheet. Drops of yellowish venom run down the side of the jar. When the "milking" is over, Barbara puts the cobra back into its case. She smiles as if to say, "It's all in a day's work."

King cobra venom is worth about three thousand dollars an ounce! Haast doesn't ship the valuable venom in its liquid form. Serpentarium workers freeze-dry the liquid. As a solid, it can be shipped anywhere it's needed.

Venom has many uses

Laboratories use most of the venom to make antivenin for saving snakebite victims. The scientists first inject horses with about one-tenth of the dose that would kill them. Every week, the dose is increased without harming the horses. After about three months, the horses are producing antibodies that destroy the venom. Their blood is then used to make the antivenin.

Other uses are being found for venom. Bill Haast began his work with the hope that snake venom would cure polio. The Salk vaccine ended that line of research, but venom has other useful properties. Venom from the Serpentarium, for example, is used to make anti-clotting drugs. These drugs help heart attack victims by preventing blood clots from forming in their arteries.

Researchers are also looking at cobra venom as a pain reliever for arthritis and cancer. Unlike other pain drugs, the venom doesn't addict the patient. It takes several weeks before it begins to work, but it works very well after it takes effect. Patients who take the diluted venom also report that they feel more cheerful.

Time for seventy-one?

As he neared his seventy-first birthday, Bill Haast counted the times he'd been bitten by cobras. When he saw that the number was an even seventy, he smiled. ''Do you suppose I'm due for another cobra bite?'' he asked.

After all those years and all those bites, Haast and other herpetologists agree on one thing. They don't believe cobras should be killed just because they're poisonous. They especially think that people should not kill cobras just to make wallets and belts from their skins. Cobras, like all snakes, play an important role in the balance of nature.

All snakes are important to the balance of nature.

MAP:

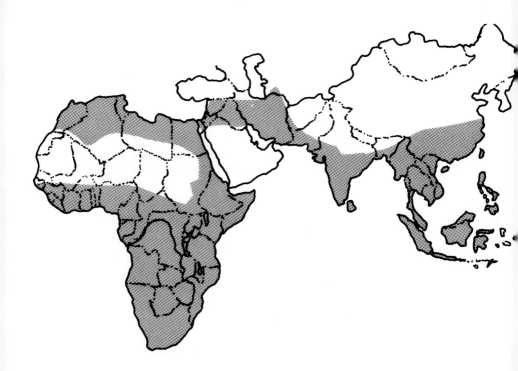

Most cobras are found within the shaded areas on this map.

INDEX/GLOSSARY:

ANTIBODIES 42, 44 — *A substance in the blood that protects the body from disease, germs or poison.*

ANTIVENIN 18, 42, 43 — *A drug that contains antibodies that protect human beings from cobra venom.*

ATTACK-DEFENSE POSTURE 22, 23, 28, 29, 32, 33, 42 — *The position a snake takes when it feels threatened. Cobras rise up, spread their hoods, hiss, and prepare to strike.*

COLD-BLOODED 14 — *Reptiles cannot control their body temperature.*

EGG TOOTH 32 — *A sharp "tooth" on a cobra's lip that it uses to cut its way out of the egg.*

FANGS 6, 9, 17, 22, 27, 29, 32, 33, 43 — *Sharp, hollow teeth that a cobra uses to inject poison into its prey.*

HABITAT 8, 13, 19, 21, 29, 39 — *The place where an animal makes its home.*

HERPETOLOGIST 18, 29, 30, 34, 38, 40, 42, 44 — *A scientist who studies snakes and other reptiles.*

JOGI 5, 6, 37 — *A snake charmer who belongs to a tribe in India that is expert in catching and handling cobras.*

MILKING 42, 43 — *The process of taking venom from a poisonous snake.*

ORGAN OF JACOBSON 17 — *A special organ in the roof of a snake's mouth which "taste-smells" material picked up on the tongue.*

PREDATOR 8, 10, 13, 33 — *An animal that lives by hunting and killing other animals.*

SCALES 9, 13, 14 — *Small, tough plates which cover and protect the skin of a cobra.*

SHIVA 36 — *A Hindu god. The cobra is one of Shiva's symbols.*

SPITTING COBRA 10, 11, 18, 19 — *A cobra that blinds its enemies or its prey by spraying venom at them from a distance.*

VENOM 6, 9, 10, 17, 18, 21, 22, 27, 29, 30, 32, 33, 41, 42, 43, 44 — *The poison used by cobras to kill their prey.*

WILDLIFE
HABITS & HABITAT

READ AND ENJOY THE SERIES:

If you would like to know more about all kinds of wildlife, you should take a look at the other books in this series.

You'll find books on bald eagles and other birds. Books on alligators and other reptiles. There are books about deer and other big-game animals. And there are books about sharks and other creatures that live in the ocean.

In all of the books you will learn that life in the wild is not easy. But you will also learn what people can do to help wildlife survive. So read on!